Ophelia

poems

V.C. Myers

Advance Praise for *Ophelia*

"In V.C. Myers' *Ophelia*, extracted from the barest bones of the Bard's language, *Hamlet*'s tragic maiden is an agent of her own magic: a *"night / witch / hallowed & gracious,"* untethered from the men of Shakespeare's play who toss her personhood around from hand to hand like a sportsball. In between the effaced monologues of Myers' erasures: poems of resistance (*"He cannot touch what we have become"*). Of the horror of nature, the horror of the flesh (*"I looked down to see the wasps / attaching their honeycombed, / fibrous nest to my lonely skin, making a new home of my body"*). Poems that reclaim the wreckage of abuse (*"let madness / grow / holy"*). Poems of resentment and outrage at a world of vultures, lined up to carve their pounds of flesh. *"It takes a village to burn a witch."* These poems are an exhale, a bloodletting—excising and displaying, as if pinned to a board in a natural history museum, the many various violences (the *"violent / fruit"*) of a world arrayed against anything unlike the recognizable. Read them."

—Chase Berggrun, author of *R E D*

"*Ophelia* is a reclamation and a wild cry, a flower of blood and ruin *"bidding goodbye to limbs / of flesh, grateful for the blossom."* In these poems, V.C. Myers draws the gothic undercurrents from Shakespeare's *Hamlet* to center Ophelia's desires, betrayals, and trauma in a series of erasures that highlights the impossible contradiction of her girlhood and pairs them with poems whose lush vibrancy shatters into violence across the page. Myers' *Ophelia* recalls the verdant rot of Millais' famous painting, Ophelia sinking into the dark currents, surrounded by riotous leaves. The beautiful is suffused with a brutality that threatens but also lures, vampiric and mesmerizing. *"In this harsh world / tell my story,"* Ophelia implores. Myers has done this and more: her *Ophelia* speaks for anyone who has breathed in the darkness and struggled to escape it."

—Elizabeth Sylvia, author of *None but Witches*

""*Belladonna served in a chipped teacup*," the poems of V.C. Myers' *Ophelia* call with siren song, pulling you into the depth of a mind filled with the torturous pain of the past, the silken whispers of a beautiful soul, the exquisite, artistic language of an intelligent mind. Filled with dark, brooding energy, dangerous, ornamental imagery, and the anger of an electric flashing warning sign, Myers has woven a tapestry of something beautiful out of darkness. Dare to let the tendrils of these poems snake around your ankles and find their way into your eyes, so they may later haunt your dreams."

—Mela Blust, author of *They Found a Woman's Body*

"V.C. Myers' *Ophelia* is a praise-song for survivors: every sacrificial virgin and trodden maiden, the Philomelas, Andromedas, #metoo women, and of course, the Ophelias. It's incantatory vengeance, festering and furious on behalf of all women who've been abused, chewed up, devoured, assaulted. Throughout the collection, Myers weaves masterful erasures from *Hamlet* that surface Ophelia's narrative, alongside the poet's own tale of survival in Appalachia where "*doe & / fawn slipped the trap,*" fleeing the huntsman. Myers bravely and honestly probes the question: How does one heal when "*trauma is a muscle memory, / [the] body longs to forget*"?"

—Dayna Patterson, author of *O Lady, Speak Again*

"*Ophelia* boldly reframes *Hamlet*, reinventing Shakespeare's tragedy with the modern world. Myers' ingenious fusion of timeless classicism and urgent societal narratives exemplifies her linguistic prowess. Every poem in this collection emerges as a lighthouse amid the tempestuous sea of self, bridging intimate experiences and universal truths. A trenchant commentary on our era. What a book!"

—Adedayo Agarau, author of *The Arrival of Rain*

"*Ophelia* is a chorus of silenced women's songs entwined, spanning centuries and literary works: Ophelia, the Little Mermaid, Philomela, Lavinia, and a contemporary woman entombed by a pandemic, society's expectations, the scars of her past. Smart, stunning, brilliant, Myers' collection is a testament to women's voices, the power imbued when we are given the space to speak."

—Jessica Drake-Thomas, author of *Burials* and *Bad Omens*

"*Ophelia* is a beautiful exploration of life and living and being, struggles and all. There are ghosts and spirits and bodies all commingling together, as if in a pot trying to figure out how to get out and live. The book deals with grief, and how to keep living, in a way that is both powerful and delicate. The use of myth and canon brings us into familiar territory in a way that is timeless and transcendent. Most of all, this book opens us all up to our vulnerabilities and imaginations, leaving us all a trail to follow."

—Joanna C. Valente, author of *η ψυχή, η ψυχή μας | the soul, our soul*

"A beautiful collection of brutal truths, Myers' *Ophelia* echoes in the hollows left by women's voices unheard."

—Lindy Ryan, author of *Bless Your Heart* and editor of *Under Her Eye* (Black Spot Books)

Ophelia

poems

V.C. Myers

Copyright © 2024 V.C. Myers

All Rights Reserved. This book or any portion thereof may not be reproduced, in whole or in part, in any form (beyond that permitted by Sections 107 and 108 of the U.S Copyright Law and except by reviewers for the public press), without the express written permission of the publisher except for the use of brief quotations in a book review.

Myers, V.C. / author

Ophelia / V.C. Myers

Poems

ISBN: 979-8-9869524-5-1

Library of Congress Control Number: 2024933626

Edited by: Elisabeth Horan
Book Design: Amanda McLeod
Cover Art: V.C. Myers, adapted from
work by John Archibald Austen
Cover Design: V.C. Myers and Amanda McLeod

PUBLISHER
Femme Salvé Books
An Imprint of Animal Heart Press
1854 Hendersonville Rd. Ste A
PMB 211
Asheville, NC 28803
www.femmesalvebooks.net
www.animalheartpress.net

for survivors

Content Warning:
non-graphic references to sexual assault & domestic violence

Foreword

We know what we are, but know not what we may be. The pulse of these poems stirs right from the epigraph, survival as a literal, the strength of its hard-won voice a new bedrock. V.C. Myers' newest work is unique, exceptional, and devastating; a direct call from that future human, gifted deep expression of the oft-unspeakable via an arsenal of mytho-literary survivors' fragments.

The profound complexity of feelings trauma survivors carry is expressed via floating bursts, flashlight soul-strobes from the character of Ophelia between the deep, stark pain of worldly and personal witness pieces. Myers' Ophelia is gossamer of self held together on the edge and still, there, is her whole made of shimmer, reflecting the poet's own deep introspection.

Myers' voice is unmistakably whole, speaking through and beyond those traumas that conspire to erase any victims' complicated unwrittens into so much blank space. The device in this collection is astonishing: the poet ferociously speaks to the refusal of that desistance via a hundred unstopped mouths, literary heroines in full fire beyond the tragedy of their known stories. Mermaid, medusa, banshee, witch, ghoul; a choir of defiant, vengeful, brink-of-broken, beautiful persisters, and between them Ophelia, and Myers herself. The blank space in the interleaved *Ophelia* erasure poems is the very opposite of silence: here it has become the poet's precision tool, delicate with rage and honing insight, hers and ours, ever sharper.

In *Sirens Chorale*, that Shakespearean epigraph becomes solid and modern. *He cannot touch what we have become*, repeats Myers, with different emphases, and that choir of survivors unashamed to speak grows enormous and present, as the #metoo movement pours out through her pen.

To let this book in, first prepare your heart for haunting – how it will stop and start in time with the ethereal, waltzing cadence of Myers' erasures, placed between clear-eyed, strikingly honest witness poems where *No imagined fear or terror can match the echo of experience.*

And always, Ophelia's blinking light, floating between unflinching narrative of trauma, the butterfly of a self battered almost to pieces over and over by storms that should never have been. If you, too, have survived the unsayable, as Ophelia does, phasing in and out from ghost-space to starkly real, may these breathtaking poems never, ever stop dancing in the dust of your closed rooms. Myers' work will hand generations the bravery and tools to find out not how experience would story them, but who they may become despite it.

This is an astonishingly deep and astute collection, poetry to draw poison from old wounds, and to Shakespeare the scars into a strong, strange, and beautiful armour that lets the wearer move free:

Lions are leaving // my skin / in scars, in droves // of / horse-drawn carriages ...

Read and read again, shed all the tears you must in the heat of anger, recognition, empathy, and catharsis – then meet the challenge this important collection places into your hands, as Myers' undeniable talent has done for all her survivorkin:

hold me // & in this harsh world / tell my story.

—Ankh Spice, author of *The Water Engine*

Table Of Contents

Ophelia	15
Ophelia	17
Papier-mâché	19
greenhouse, glasshouse, it's all the same & broken	20
Ophelia	22
Backwoods Bloodletting	24
Disintegration	25
Ophelia	26
Exile is Not a Street Address	28
Fire-tongued Labyrinth	30
Ophelia	32
Formative	34
Avaricious Symbiosis	35
Ophelia	36
No Trespassing	38
Scarecrow	39
Ophelia	40
Labor of Love	42
Ventriloquy	43
Ophelia	44
Birds of Prey	46
Metamorphosis	48
Ophelia	50
Ophelia	52
American Gothic	54
Hunting Ground	56
Ophelia	58
Whistleblower	60
In Search of a Karass	61
Ophelia	63
Andromeda Awaits the Kraken	65
Exile	67
Ophelia	68
Midnight in the City	70

Pulp	71
Ophelia	72
Blood Thicket	74
Prelude to Keening	76
Ophelia	79
Sirens Chorale	81
Masterpiece	82
Ophelia	83
The Phoenix Rises (More Fog than Fire)	85
Geometries of Benediction	86
Ophelia	88
Ophelia	90
Ophelia Playlist	92
End Notes	93
Acknowledgements	94
About the Author	96

We know what we are, but know not what we may be.

- William Shakespeare, *Hamlet*

Hell is other people.

- Jean-Paul Sartre, *No Exit*

Ophelia

            unfold yourself
carefully
      sick
            star
  burn
                with fear &
                wonder

strange
strange
      night

              hot &
lawless &
lost

   star   of fire &   blood

              Neptune's empire
      sick   with eclipse

harbinger

        omen

                      ghost

  in sea or fire, in earth or air

                night

     witch

hallowed & gracious

Ophelia

      sister

             sleep

          sweet

                  temple

            of fear

     the yielding

     the song

your heart

your danger

             unmask   the moon

reckless libertine

                          beware

                    beware

  the night

                        remember
                    tender
        blood   burns

                        prodigal
                                daughter
    fire
        maiden

                        unholy
breath
                sanctified

Papier-mâché

I befriended the red paper wasps
flying around my garden. I sang
as they circled me. I watered the
flowers they pollinated. Such
camaraderie, such peace Such
subtle symbiosis. Eventually I
no longer noticed them. I forgot
they were ever there. When I
felt a strange weight on my leg,
I looked down to see the wasps
attaching their honeycombed,
fibrous nest to my lonely skin,
making a new home of my body.
I watched the nest grow bigger,
consuming one leg, then the other,
swaddling all of my limbs, creeping
up my torso like an invasive vine
curling around a dying tree. The nest
cocooned my throat so I couldn't
breathe, sealed my mouth so I couldn't
scream, covered my eyes so I couldn't
see what too much trust made of me.

greenhouse, glasshouse, it's all the same & broken

    Pronounce the moon an aperture, I'll wait.
The sound of bells & locusts emerging from
the ground. I know you want me raw, spread out
on the page, but I've already been eaten by
everyone I encountered today. Every person I meet
says smile more, but I've learned smiling
is seen as an invitation. I prefer to be
a closed door & locked.
    People keep trying to kill me
with their unvaccinated children & backyard
chickens, their denial of climate change &
affordable healthcare. A chronic, toxic bloom
of flowers emerging from
my body, buds bursting from
my mouth, ivy curling from
my ears, my skin cracked glass, the sky ceiling
of a hothouse, my blood boiling from
mysterious fevers misdiagnosed
for years by white coat indifference.

Doctors simply shrug, reaching for-
ward, ripping   the petals from
my pores,   dismissing me,   insisting
        it was all in my head.
So go on, keep asking. I'll keep drinking
& pretending   that my father is alive
& never hit my mother;   that I was loved
& wanted & never homeless; that every friend
I've ever had was never beaten or raped; that I am
light & thin & pretty & have never seriously
considered suicide   multiple times   since I was
a little girl   watching   my father   hit my mother.
I don't mind aging, because I'm still running
from my past. I started drinking   to forget
he was alive. I kept drinking   to forget
he was dead. I stopped drinking   to let
the memories do what they must.
Everyone promises time will heal my wounds, but
gaslight is not antiseptic. They all want a Band-Aid
over what I need   to fester.
        Trauma is a muscle memory,
my body longs to forget.

Ophelia

       sorrow

            sister

surrender

   head   heart

      the throne of

             dread

your coronation

         confess

         consent

    solemn

      suspiration of   breath

 the   river

               of grief

    sweet nature

        mourning

            lost

    sorrow

shows

a heart unfortified

            earthly thunder

      sullied flesh

            self-slaughter

        an unweeded garden

her face   heaven & earth

     she
    the dead
           appears
    fear
    the apparition

          strange

&
             amazed

Backwoods Bloodletting

Battling his legacy, the child liberates mercy,
making a new fashion of kindness, burning
bridges of damnation. Witness the birth of
estrangement. Tenderness rising of ashes. Her
bare feet clear a new path in the forest. Trees on
mountainsides bleed red waterfalls in protest.
Sacrilegious flesh, a veil, a dress worn only for
special occasions, tattered, a Sisyphean weight
I drag as I await death. My view of mud,
my mountaintop hermitage, a prayer. How
slithering is breathing, being, a waste. Accursed
inheritance, an affliction. Seed sunken too far
to sprout, to grow. Darkness devours daylight,
withering the untended garden. Split cocoon,
premature wings, captured under glass & set afire.
Bury my eyes beside my grandmother's grave, so
I can see remnants of love. Ripping nightshade off
my throat, a scream for clarity. Bare bones & old
photos, all lies. Sick spinning on your turntable,
a bitter melody of ghosts in your parlor. Sing sorry,
sew your illusions, a cover for someone else's bed.

Disintegration

The dead rose up before me, to keep me company,

a ghost dance of fallow friendship.

Heathens rarely get invited to dinner here.

We're expected to display gratitude for any crumb

fallen from the faithful table. Inquisition is

in season, a party planned by patriarchy.

The castle keep is full tonight.

The dungeon offers a more panoramic view.

What lovely monsters we are, shunned for our dark splendor.

Paradise's fruit rots beneath our dirty boots.

Serpents slither, my Medusa hair.

I crawl, belly on floor, begging for

some more, some morsel of mercy.

Trust is a broken gate. Gatekeepers gaslight all complaints.

Zookeepers never unlock their cages.

Under these floorboards, I curl up & imagine

I see stars where dim light creeps in through the cracks.

It takes a village to burn a witch.

Blood on their hands like sour wine.

Ophelia

        an eager air
            draws near
                  the spirit
  marrow of
        grace,
           corrupt

                    enter ghost
angel
      or goblin
           heaven or
hell

     wicked
        bones
    burst   the sepulcher
               jaws
          of the moon
                        beckon
beckon
be   immortal as
  waves

       you   the flood
                               the cliff
                               the sea
assume some other   form
                                            madness
                  fathoms   the sea
& hears it roar
                       waves
    your
           fate
                       this body
      called

Exile is Not a Street Address

A silver, kinetic sculpture of a tree
planted in the city park's pavement
sways its metallic branches as the
winter wind swirls snow in circles,
frosting the empty gray sidewalks.
I put down new roots, my veins, in
stone after fleeing the floods of home.
My skin cracks & peels, but still
I refuse to yield to the drought.
Unbidden solitude offers no peace.
Church bells toll, but not to lull me.
A car horn signals, but not to lure me.
A window closes to my cold stare.
Is this what death feels like, but still
bound in flesh? A ghost gift-wrapped
in skin. How odd to mourn oneself.
Dry, detested bones drink dust in
the archives of neglect. My hands
retreat from reaching out, clenching
fists when no one clasps my open palm.

Sleeping with a light on for company,
I wake up screaming when nightmares
mimic memories. No imagined fear or
terror can match the echo of experience.
At the conductor's condemning cue,
the symphony strikes a somber note.
A dirge for my unhallowed exit.

Fire-tongued Labyrinth

I was born in a blue field
after the circus
        came to town.

    Doves flew
from my sister's throat as
she swallowed   bright
        stars.

            The stag
rested   in the hunter's horn,
sounding out   sour notes of
        kudzu.

Fireflies have no faith
        nor need of
sun & fluorescent
    bulbs.

       Whisper

indoors, the walls

              have ears & flies

stuck   in their ointment.

Lions are leaving

              my skin

in scars, in droves   of

      horse-drawn carriages.

Ophelia

                              enter ghost
               lead
                         tormenting
                  spirit
  doomed   to walk
                              in fires

               harrow   blood
                    stars
                         & blood

                    strange
                              love

          sleeping orchard
  serpent
               of death
                         beast
  wicked
               love
                    radiant

  prey

                sleeping   orchard

                                            blood
                                            blood
                                            blossoms   sin

                        thorns
                                of
                                    hell
                                            grow
    in
                                        memory

Formative

The teacher lured
the class with
lollipops, marching
them, single-file,
to the cemetery.
Haunting takes
so many forms,
lingering like the
bitter aftertaste
of sour hard candy
swallowed in a field
of unmarked graves.

Avaricious Symbiosis

Axiom breath of dead lungs, the calm
bombastic births a delicate cacophony.
Imagine the illusion of incandescence,
mesmeric, effulgence over a chasm.
Juxtapose an artless, xenophobic
greeting, devoid of empathy, with a fire
-fighter holding a child in an old photograph.
How far beneath us is gratitude, dignity
of language, of verbal silk?
Can a knife be neutral in any hand?
Farewell my kaleidoscopic forgiveness,
reality supersedes trust underneath the bruise.
Yonder is the last civilization
in a zoo no one cares to visit.

Ophelia

you

                    drift

                              near

                                    him

     wanton, wild, &

       open

               breathe his faults

you

                    drift

      laying

         soiled

            breath   of guilt

            this consequence

of man

            the consequence

               the consequence

   falling out
       of reach

mad for   love
   his face
       his eyes
  the last   light

      desperate
         mad
 beyond
   discretion

more grief to

come

No Trespassing

A small, solitary carousel horse stands
impaled on a rusted pole
tangled in barbed wire & tall grass,
decayed by flood water & mud,
its black paint peeled away, revealing
a white plastic skull, one-eyed &
screaming.

Scarecrow

> *My girl, my girl, don't lie to me. Tell me, where did you sleep last night? In the pines, in the pines, where the sun don't ever shine.*
>
> -Lead Belly

In the end, we will only remember the girl   in a field of negligence,
   crows plucking   eyes from a scarecrow, the girl,
   crows plucking   her eyes, her innocence,
   crows plucking   her heart-strings   like a dulcimer,
   crows plucking   her heart out   in time with the melody,
   crows   & the scarecrow girl—
               a heart plucked in time,
               a heartbeat   at a time—
    a girl, a scarecrow, a girl-
crow plucked   by her own kind   in time.

We'll remember the girl, & the field   of crows,
       & a boy,
          a shotgun,
              singing harmony   from a distance.

Ophelia

                              not living

                                    will please you,

you hope

            your dread pleasures
            that great feast
               dear death

madness   is art

        doubt stars
        doubt sun
        doubt love

                 ill daughter

                       kissing carrion

                      daughter
          speak   madness &
leave him
            leave you

                                the world
a dream
          a shadow

            your discovery
                                golden fire
            your death
            your bounty

               mad   & free

Labor of Love

*A mermaid has no tears, and therefore
she suffers so much more.*

- Hans Christian Anderson, *The Little Mermaid*

The Little Mermaid's tongue & tail traded

                for a pair of legs & a prince's eye.

Syrinx, a river reed plucked   to serve

                as padding for Pan's lecherous pipes.

        Sweet music made of mute women.

                We always talk of his burden.
Sisyphus shoving stone up & down the mountain every day.

                            Poor guy.

No one pities the stone.

                She got herself into that mess.

Ventriloquy

> *Lavinia, ravished; her hands cut off, her tongue cut out.*
>
>   - Shakespeare, *Titus Andronicus*

He stole my tongue in Spring   to seal
my witness mouth,   sawed off
my plaintiff hands,   so I'll not *play*
the cook nor feast   on vengeance pie.

I shall teach myself once more
to speak   without my tongue,
to feel   without my fingers.

Such horrors visited upon
my muted skin,
this pile   of butchered flesh,
this pyre   of sacrificial wood.

                 Let my stumps *play*
the scribe & paint   in blood
every scream   he denied me.

Ophelia

      you   drift

    turbulent & dangerous

   wild

         lone

              sea

                  end

the heartache

           dream of

          death

         shuffle off this mortal coil

          death,

the undiscovered

           current

              —nymph

                    your beauty

               will soon

  transform

            love

              made you

  a   sinner

                                    crawling

between earth & heaven

    you sweet plague

                       mad

                 wretched

         honey

       sweet bell   jangled, out of time

          melancholy

        seas

sprung from

    madness

Birds of Prey

> *Philomela is mutilated...They are transformed into birds.*
>
> - Ovid, *Metamorphoses*

He cut so much of me,
ripped out   my voice
        to silence me.

My secret sorrow shared,
a tale of terror   woven
into a gifted tapestry.

Seeking sisterly solace,
swift swallow's sacrifice
baked a cruel revenge.

   A most horrid feast
further festers fresh wounds.
Fists shaken at sky sprout

furious wings.   Reborn, we
became birds of night, flying
far   beyond the beastly stars,

Callisto's cursed constellation,

a family forever   divided

& flung   across the heavens.

Metamorphosis

> *Daphne becomes the laurel bough...*
> *he driven by desire, she by fear.*

- Ovid. Metamorphoses

He dared to call it love.   Blind
to her desperation.   No romance
in his relentless pursuit, his hands
so desperate for plunder.

Her only escape was prayer, begging
for transformation, as grief hardened
the tears of Phaeton's sisters into amber
& bent their bodies into poplar trees.

When gnarled branches grew skyward
from her ravaged torso, she sighed
in relief, bidding goodbye to limbs
of flesh, grateful for the blossom

of bark upon her skin, for laurel leaves
sprouting in her hair, silk tresses turning
to twigs, tendrils of rough wood building
a kindred nest for wounded birds.

Ophelia

                torrent, tempest
        whirlwind   her body
             the theater of others
        blood & judgment so well
                a brute part to kill
              memory
                      a church of
                      the dead

Neptune's salt moon
                    sacred
    the sun & moon
      fear & love
         wormwood
                      kiss
  violent
       fruit
  violence of
          grief
               grief
                    grief

    earth

    an anchor

    the tedious day

        withers

                raven

thoughts black

                      creature of

                midnight

        poison garden

            forest of   affliction

obey

    your liberty

    your grief

    your compass

        the witching night

                breathes

                          hot

blood

Ophelia

let madness

                                                              grow

   holy

                fear
              feed on

                          the mind

  die alone

              small

                    ruin

                            alone

                    this voyage

                    this fear

             primal

                                    blood

                      the sweet

crown

            corrupted current

the wicked prize

the true nature

                        the teeth of

                                    death

                        full of bread

the purging

              passage

                        a horrid bed

American Gothic

> *She was not a Respectable Married Woman*
> *but fully a human being.*
>
> - Sinclair Lewis, *Main Street*

In the mountains of Appalachia / at the dead end / of a muddy holler / stands / a derelict farmhouse / where weathered hands / & calloused hearts / mold / a hardened, rotted monstrosity / from the delicate clay / of matrimony. // He lives / in a perpetual state / of shrug, / tasting / neither the sweetness / of joy / nor the bitter bite / of sorrow. / He chews / her self-worth / with razor sharp teeth, / cruel words / further bruise / her already battered skin. / Insult added to injury. // Scraps of Scripture / floating in mid-air; / her hidden Bible burst / into a holy cloud / of confetti, / torn by hand / for his ticker tape parade; // settling softly, silently / beneath their violent embrace. / He, the Hunter, / mounts his trophy / to the wall, / his steel trap fists / locked / around her wrists. // Caught, / she, his captive / prey, / his trembling doe. / The eyewitness, / their hybrid fawn, / rent asunder / by their woodcut / *danse macabre*. //

Fearing his mercurial wrath, / his hair-trigger shotgun, / doe & fawn slipped the trap, / backwoods refugees / fleeing flesh & blood. // They rest / in a hidden hollow, / a shelter / of sympathy. / The fawn cradled / in strange arms / as its mother awaits judgement / on unforgiving, // dirty Welfare chairs / carved of yellow plastic, / a modern snare. / Doe transformed / to domestic, / hired help / for pampered patrons / of the poor. // Her new perfume: / the smell of bleach. / A scent / so clean / he could not track. / A trail / so cold / he dare not follow.

Hunting Ground

He hunts in fields of secrecy. She wilds in his crosshairs.
He corners, she falls through time. Charon waives his fee
to usher her to safety. She hides among the River Styx reeds,
between the world & the underworld, the waking & the dead,
a system of forgotten stars. Our excuses betray our motives.
He chases shadows & shades, echoes of past crimes.
Rivers part like open legs   to succor her escape.
Devour kingly monuments, his legacy of lies.
Pandora's box is brimming with his victims.   Hope
fled long ago.   Innocence is an endangered species.
How soiled the linens   of thievery. Combat
under black tie. Divinity knows not bruised flesh.
Mountains take her in. He stalks the riverbank.
I crescent to demonstrate   her muffled screams,
amplified, multiplied, in shafts of light, of revelation—
the prized hind in hushed tones,   gaslit & filed away,
viral royal art collusion, the old guard's resurrected blade,
flowers laid on graves   of sacrament,
the forest's eyes are closed   to her desecration,
ivy curling to obscure, talons sprouting from stumps,
a country empty   of nurture.

We weeping willow hang, sickened,   the sea gives up
its dead,   the river plays coy, feigning ignorance.
How dark the sound of greed   in a state of emergency, emergent.
He scouts ahead for witnesses, she runs
to fall again   on wobbly promises of future justice.
Blood for blood   would be a relief.

Ophelia

the rood

the queen

                a bloody deed

                a bloody deed

kill a king

kill a king

                wring your hands

                wring your heart

the blush of

the rose

                an innocent love

the glow

the doom

the herald kiss

        this fair mountain

        this moor

                call it love

the blood

the judgment

                    madness

  rebellious fire

        burn

       black &

       rank

   corruption honey

           ecstasy

the empire

the rule

the precious diadem

        wild blood

the portal

the creation

           ecstasy

         ecstasy

   madness madness madness

  a monster

  a wondrous grave

Whistleblower

Do what you are going to do, and I will tell about it.

- Sharon Olds

Her mouth is a sinkhole / swallowing / your hometown / as you serenely sip tea / at a garden party / or ride / a Ferris wheel / with your sweetheart. / Blissful ignorance / always ends / in total destruction. // All fairy tales were born / of great horror. / Sleeping Beauty's rape / by her beloved prince / satiated salacious storytellers for centuries / long before / Polanski's champagne, / Ceelo's ecstasy / & Cosby's cappuccino chorus line / danced / the opening number / for King Weinstein's sleazy headlines. // Monsters wear masks / of men's faces / as their hands & teeth / unroll old B-movie reels / of secret shame— / all scratches / & out-of-sync audio. / Convert to video / & upload to YouTube. / Her terror / is #trending. // Stagnant mosquito ponds pool / in her vacant eyes, / in his violent wake. // Defense mechanisms / are fragile shields / before the inevitable trauma / of new reality / comes crashing / into existence, / ripping out / into grotesque shapes— / bloody gargoyle births. // All we can do now / is help her / wrap / the police tape / back across / her mouth / around the crime scene / he made / of her body.

In Search of a Karass

a karass ignores national, institutional, occupational, familial,
and class boundaries

- Kurt Vonnegut, Jr., *Cat's Cradle*

The carcass
                lays
                                sprawled
    across a mist-
        cloaked field.

Mildewed tents, rusty
            cages, the bones
    of an abandoned
carnival,   'twined in dead
                grass & discarded serpent skin.

      When unchecked weeds, wild &
carnivorous, swallowed
                sad
children whole, neighbors   turned
                          their faces away.

One man's indifference is another's shame. Blame
passes   through every set of lips
       until the next bite.

Drops of blood
            on a snowdrift,
                     in my palms on the wheel, driving
                     cross-country to reach
ocean, my spleen   a piece of sea
                         glass.   Still,
       it shall be vented.

Ophelia

                      sigh

mad sea

                              stir

        this apprehension

        the unseen
        threat

        this bloody deed

will

    haunt

                our love

the sun

the mountain

the chapel

        whisper

the air

        of discord

                          dead
                                    kin
                   demand

the end
                          the jaw
            of
                nothing

Andromeda Awaits the Kraken

Shivering in sea air, shackled to this rock,
my floral crown in carnage, a whirlwind of
petals, cloud of breath, morbid bloom of regret.

Of latitude, I seek sanctuary in shadow.
Of longitude, I seek sanguinity in surrender.

I crave kindred, kinetic connectivity, alternating
currents of Tesla coil kisses, electromagnetic
oscillation, a high voltage time travel liaison.

I am spoiled silk, wine-stained & drowning.
Heavy cream churned & whipped, mason jarred &
shelved. Farcical agony, Greek tragedy spawn.

For a mother's sinful boast, I become a banquet for
a sea monster. I need no Gorgon-wielding savior,
no garland of stars, no posthumous constellation.

Gather ye rosebuds, your storm of thorns.
Gather together to pray, to dance, to mourn.

I current at dawn, I tide at dusk, twilight, my reprieve.

I, the bounty of jackals. I, the sacrificial lamb.

In your mouth, I am reborn.

Exile

> *Although the villagers had forgotten the ritual...*
> *they still remembered to use stones.*
>
> - Shirley Jackson, *The Lottery*

Your hollow affability
reduces me   to this tenuous form.

A weak rendering, devoid of substance,
a brittle avatar of malevolent images
flashing   through your distorted mind.

My insurrection, a sacrilege
in your constricted perception.

Your rapacious appetite for righteousness
devours   my humanity.

I am your preternatural creation.

The beast of condemnation.

Ophelia

                    seek

            danger

                    deliberate

                                      desperate

  desperate

the dead

            know your pleasure

a certain convocation of

        creatures

    maggots

                              fed of

                                a king

   the guts of

            heaven

   tender

        flesh

                raw & red

the sword, &

    sovereign

              death

hectic   blood   rages

    joy

Midnight in the City

Dirty hostel broken lock
bathroom slaughterhouse
splattered communal filth

Psycho stranger across
the hall ranting about
bar brawls & evil sluts

Awaits the mothership
with his "One World
Leader" lapel badge

Wanna go?

Pulp

   Night terror
architecture ascending
from your bed   of nails,
a pillow   of blood   red
roses, ripped   petals, thorny
talons clawing,   a knife-
   kissed cheek.

   Plums ripened in
rib cage,   lungs full of
bloody juices,   cut
out   the heartseed,   tied
in sinew strings,   voice
choking   on brambles,
   a silent scream.

Ophelia

       army of

         a promised kingdom

the majesty

                power

                  of

                  command

the frontier

the garrison

                of

                man

              a beast

    made

           godlike

    bestial oblivion

                craven

                earth

    witness this army of

                  divine ambition

            mortal

                  danger

           at the stake

                      stand

                      stained

                              blood

& shame

imminent death

  a fantasy

            graves like beds

       tomb enough

to hide   from

              thought

Blood Thicket

Red horns wrapped in fur on a battered wall.
Claw out my entrails with a fine-tooth comb.
Sinew & tendon, gristle & feast.
Rotting intestines in meat market heat.
Sucked to the marrow, ribcage cathedral.
Under your floorboards, I shudder to think.
Gather the cradles, we'll use them as bait.
Seize the scythe maiden, her harp left unstrung.
Hobgoblin cruelty, grackles cackle of sin.
Kiss the black widow, red hourglass tongue.
Garland of serpents, a night without end.
Cellar of cadence, how cold, how mighty.
Song of cicada, your schism of sighs.
Bridge to your burrow, just out of my reach.
Fodder for wolf pack, sweet nectar of spit.
Tangle til morning, my starless nightgown.
Vows of repentance will not save you now.
Belladonna served in a chipped teacup.
Paint your teeth onyx & unhinge your jaws.
Torches in hindsight, pale steed, take your leave.
Nest of kin vipers, I swear it will hurt.

Screams caught bell jar, ax stuck in the door.

Black market kidney, your bathtub brims blood.

Organ grinder waltz, lips sewn by black thread.

Rigamortis charm, your beloved is dead.

Haunted my carnival, your grotesque sideshow.

Trembling, my circus. Violence, your art.

Prelude to Keening

Banshee knows   where your eyeballs go   every night
when you dream.
       She whispers.   She whispers.   She whispers.
Your only warning—   a susurrus hiss,   a quiet crinkle like
paper   dolls, tearing,   a sundering rip.   She straddles
your chest,   her vicious vise grip.   She hums & thrums
       her thighs,   your lungs, her drum
your ribs,   her harp,   unstrung.
A macabre melody,   an eerie intro to   her somnolent
       serenade,   her lullaby cry,
her spectacular, spectral scream.
       She's crafty   in the dark,   sewing
at the midnight hour,   her fine needle   threaded with
       razor wire—   stitching
       your mouth,
her crooked, bloody seam.
       Grotesque her visage,   you adore her
bulging, bloodshot eyes, her protruding, putrescent tongue,
rotting & rough,   she'll lick your skin   raw
as you sleep.   She, the succubus,
       you, her succulent
    treat.

      You'd scream, too,
              in such employment, but
a ghoul's
  gotta   eat & you smell ripe enough.
The stink of you,   her new favorite perfume.
      Gruesome, her grasp,   her hanging hag hair,
a shroud of woe on   your winter bed.
She warms up her voice, a cacophonous scale,
          an echo of
                discordant dread.
        O, glorious scream!
We eagerly await   your marvelous, monstrous
birth.
                But first,
she'll hollow you out—a flesh shell, a ringing bell
calling her
         to worship,   to sing.
She feels your surrender coming, the cutting cold,
         the howling wind,
    your slipstream   into oblivion.
    Your death rattle,   her tambourine.
        The last song.   Her last kiss.
She seals your bed   into a sarcophagus.

Your ghastly bride,	your defrocked priest,	your
	malevolent morphine drip release.
	The time for
reckoning	has come.
	O, glorious scream!
   Your ghost,	her spawn.

Ophelia

mood   beats her
                                     heart

           her words

dangerous

           her sick soul   sin's toy

Ophelia sings   love is
               a headstone

Ophelia sings
                       we know what we are
                       but not what we may be

she will choose cold
                 the poison of deep grief

     sorrows come
     in battalions
                    violent
                        thoughts &
whispers

                    poor Ophelia
                divided   from herself

        beasts come
          in clouds
                    to infect
        with pestilent speeches

                                        noise within
the messenger
the riot
the cry

                                        noise within
the false trail
the false door

                    what is
            divinity
                damnation

                                        noise within
                madness
                        madness

Sirens Chorale

> *me too*
>
> - Tarana Burke

> *If all the women who have been sexually harassed or assaulted wrote 'Me too' as a status, we might give people a sense of the magnitude of the problem*
>
> - Alyssa Milano

He cannot touch   what we have become.

He cannot **touch**   what we have **become**.

He cannot touch   what **We** have become.

He cannot touch what we have become.
He cannot touch what we have become.
He cannot touch what we have become.

HE CANNOT TOUCH WHAT WE HAVE BECOME.

Masterpiece

Her hips undulate carnelian fire.

      Her hair splashes cerulean sea.

           Her belly births blue sky.

           Her palms plant tones of earth,

     brown, yellow, green grass

sprouts from her flicking wrist.

She stomps scarlet, bending

      to kiss the wild canvas

           her body brought to life.

Ophelia

Gravedigger, Gravedigger,

                    is she buried

salvation, her grave

the crown, her burial

Gravedigger, Gravedigger,

                    she drowned herself

the water

the water

the water   drown, drown

the truth, buried

this world, a heathen

the scripture, the scripture

the gallows

the gallows

the gallows

the gallows

                        sweet skull, skull sweet

                        sweet lord, these bones

    a pit of skulls

    mad dirty shovel full

    parchment made of skin

Sing   O, a pit of the dead,

              she's dead

              strange

              strange

                        mad skull kissed

    winter's queen, the corpse of Ophelia

    the Queen of death

    the maiden of bell & burial

    the dead sing a requiem to her

    fair & unpolluted flesh

violets spring howling   the fair Ophelia

she scatters flowers   the sky

            the stars

                      wonder-wounded

The Phoenix Rises (More Fog than Fire)

Leaving earth, I know,

in between screams,

land was too hard for me

to move forward.

An antiquated calm,

rusting stagnation.

After, ether,

I descend   like a mist,

thump tin roofs, crawl downspouts, tangle

in orb weaver webs & garden hoses,

winding them with water snakes

into a noose,

so I won't have to survive

another winter   in these haunted woods.

Eerie whispers shake the sycamore trees

& the graves have all cracked open.

The cove is calling

for a new sacrifice,

but I have nothing left

to give.

Every moon whispers

don't go...

Geometries of Benediction

Hidden, she, of cloven hoof, kicking fire,
devours the fog-cloaked mountaintops, rustles
burnished bronze dreams fallen, broken,
ritual sacrifices offered on Autumn's altar.

Two young bucks lock antlers, fighting for
dominance, while the world refracts like a
crushed prism, kaleidoscopic & lost.

Milk spilt on shattered glass, domestic shards.

Skyscraper remorse desiccated in desert sun,
your certainty trembles in thimble time. In
situ tableau, a morgue of truth, what contempt,
what grace, a form of recompense, a river spent.

Softly, softly, the soil indents over a grave.
Starlings, a grackle, a rattle, a snake. Away,
we explore the geometries of benediction.

Shimmering insects, my kin, burrow beneath
my skin, growing roots in my veins. We trees,
bent, dark, twisted, monstrous—adore us.
Excess of sound, a song, a chorus of skeletons,
bones of my innocence, my sepulchral youth.

Breathing in orbit, the atmospheric wake, empty
of malice, of mercy, I taste
sweet destruction—our holy, our god.

Ophelia

        nature   stirred
     virtue or plague
she is
      the star   in his sphere
the great love
the spring

   lost sister   driven   into sleep
   shook with   love, love
                 sudden
                              &
              strange
 this witchcraft
       wondrous
              the painting of a sorrow,
love, love
              the spark & fire
  the sword
  the moon
  the death

sister   drowned, drowned
                          a willow   in the glassy stream
                          with fantastic garlands of
   crows

     cold maid
        mermaid   of distress
  a creature   & element
                   heavy with drink
                   her melodious, muddy death
she is drowned, drowned, drowned
too much water,
        poor Ophelia

   adieu,
            o' fire that drowns

Ophelia

sleep

      deep divinity

sea-gown, the dark, unfold

      goblin

            stay the ax

  a prologue to

    love

                her garland of death

  the changeling

sea-fight   nature incensed

  beast of beasts

cold wind

cold breath

             the dagger

                      madness

              madness

     madness

           my revenge

                she lifts the cup

the poisoned cup

                the queen falls

    the drink, the dr_nk

        poison

the treacherous ins=rument

        venom

            venom

            death come

                death,
        hold me

& in this harsh world
    tell my story.

Ophelia Playlist

https://sptfy.com/opheliabook

End Notes

All quoted works are in the public domain:

Ophelia erasure series source text: *Hamlet* by William Shakespeare

Ventriloquy: Quotes from *Titus Andronicus* by William Shakespeare

Andromeda Awaits the Kraken: Quote by Robert Herrick

Acknowledgements

Endless gratitude to *Femme Salvé* editors Amanda McLeod, Beth Gordon, and Elisabeth Horan. I cannot imagine more loving or talented hands to have placed this book in. Thank you for inspiring me, believing in my work, and taking me in when I most needed it. You are truly a gift to the poetry community.

Thank you to Ankh Spice and Adedayo Agarau, my dearest poet friends. Your kindness and your poetry never fail to amaze me. It was a privilege to work with you both at *Barren*, it's been a blessing to have you in my life and my heart ever since.

Thank you to my Shakespeare sisters, Dayna Patterson and Elizabeth Sylvia, for inviting me into your Bard coven. Thanks also to all the other poets who have given their time, insight, and support to this book: Mela Blust, Joanna Valente, Jessica Drake-Thomas, and Kristin Garth.

A special thanks to Chase Berggrun, whose book R E D and thoughtful approach to erasure poetry were deeply influential in the making of *Ophelia*.

Variations of some poems first appeared in the book, *Give the Bard a Tetanus Shot* (Vegetarian Alcoholic Press, 2019) or in the following literary journals:

Bohème
Bowery Gothic
Coffin Bell
Dream Pop Journal
Entropy
Feral
Five:2:One
Isele Magazine
Marvelous Verses Anthology (The Daily Drunk Press)
Minola Review
OyeDrum Magazine
Poet Lore
For RAINN Benefit Album (audio recording)
Rogue Agent
Southword
The Chestnut Review
The Galway Review
The Lost Library (Pink Plastic House Press)
The Maine Review
They Call Us Bossy
Yes Poetry

About the Author

V.C. Myers is the author of *Ophelia* (Femme Salvé Books, 2023) and *Give the Bard a Tetanus Shot* (Vegetarian Alcoholic Press, 2019). She has edited for *Barren Magazine*, the *New International Voices* series (Ice Floe Press), and *Frontier Poetry*. Her work has appeared in ekphrastic exhibits and journals worldwide, including *EPOCH*, *Poet Lore*, *Prairie Schooner*, *The Minnesota Review*, *The Galway Review*, and *Feral*. An Appalachian poet, she has lived in Ireland, England, and West Virginia. Her website is vcmyers.com.

www.ingramcontent.com/pod-product-compliance
Lightning Source LLC
Chambersburg PA
CBHW071121160426
43196CB00013B/2662